CORONET

40 mm · 100 mm · 560 mm · 150 mm · 95 mm · 70 mm · 50 mm · glue

KV-232-511

CROWN

60 mm · 56 mm · 560 mm · 25 mm · glue

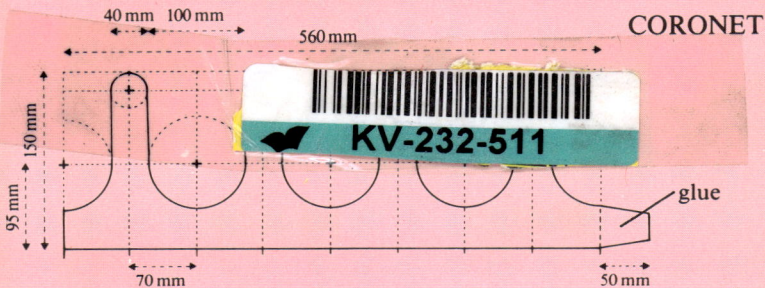

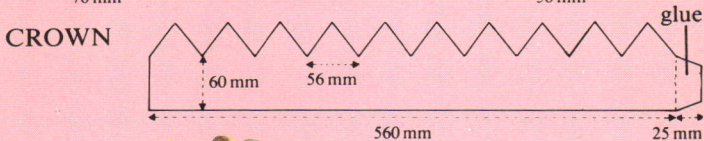

MANDARIN'S HAT

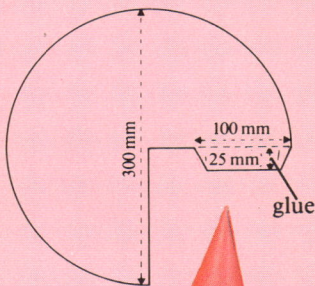

300 mm · 100 mm · 25 mm · glue

Contents

First edition

© LADYBIRD BOOKS LTD MCMLXXXII

Party Games

by DAPHNE TIBBITT and DIANA UNDERWOOD
photographs by TIM CLARK and JOHN MOYES

Ladybird Books Loughborough

Planning a Party

The key words of a successful party, for any age, are colour and planning. For young guests hang bunches of balloons in doorways, on the banisters (well out of reach) and from picture hooks. Use some of the smaller balloons for games, keeping the biggest to send home with each child (plus a few spares for brothers and sisters!)

For three to five year olds, it is a good idea to provide a 'container' for each child with his or her name on it, in which hankies and prizes can be placed. (This avoids any arguments at the end over who had what!) Decorated paper bags or egg box lids covered with coloured paper make excellent containers.

Prizes are always a problem, but need not be expensive if you keep them simple. A selection of sweets attractively arranged on a plate from which each child chooses his own 'prize' is an easy solution. You may feel that certain games merit something of a slightly higher value to the winner, but for the very young, make sure that no one goes home empty handed.

Small children lack concentration for elaborate games but will play musical games tirelessly. They often want to repeat the same game a number of times. The tunes, words and actions are mainly traditional.

Games
for THREE
to FOUR
year olds

Here We Go Round the Mulberry Bush

The children join hands and skip round in a ring to the first verse, then suit the actions to the words for verses two to five. Then they repeat verse one, skipping round in a ring again.

Here we go round the mul-berry bush, The mul-berry bush, the mul-berry bush,

Here we go round the mul-berry bush , on a cold and frost - y morn - ing.

Here we go round the mulberry bush,
The mulberry bush, the mulberry bush,
Here we go round the mulberry bush
On a cold and frosty morning.

This is the way we wash our hands,
Wash our hands, wash our hands,
This is the way we wash our hands
On a cold and frosty morning.

This is the way we dry our hands.
Dry our hands, dry our hands,
This is the way we dry our hands
On a cold and frosty morning.

This is the way we clap our hands,
Clap our hands, clap our hands,
This is the way we clap our hands
On a cold and frosty morning.

This is the way we warm our hands,
Warm our hands, warm our hands,
This is the way we warm our hands
On a cold and frosty morning.

Repeat verse one.

Nuts in May

Form the children into two lines facing each other and holding hands. The lines advance and retreat alternately, singing the first two verses.

During the singing of verse three the first line chooses a member of the opposite line to be Nuts in May, at the same time nominating their own player to 'pull her away' in verse five.

Here we come gathering nuts in May,
Nuts in May, nuts in May,
Here we come gathering nuts in May
On a cold and frosty morning.

Who will you have for nuts in May,
Nuts in May, nuts in May,
Who will you have for nuts in May
On a cold and frosty morning?

We'll have . . . . . for nuts in May,
Nuts in May, nuts in May,
We'll have . . . . . for nuts in May
On a cold and frosty morning.

Who will you send to pull her away,
Pull her away, pull her away,
Who will you send to pull her away,
On a cold and frosty morning?

We'll send . . . . . to pull her away,
Pull her away, pull her away,
We'll send . . . . . to pull her away,
On a cold and frosty morning.

Here we come gath er - ing nuts in May, nuts in May, nuts in May, Here we come gath er - ing nuts in May, on a cold and fros – ty morn – ing.

The game continues until all the players have been pulled to one side.

Ring a Ring o' Roses

This is one of the oldest and best loved rhymes. There are several versions depending on the age of your guests. Very young children will love jumping about then falling down on a cushion at the appropriate time. Older children may like to form a circle and dance round, perhaps suggesting that the last player 'down' is also out.

Ring a ring o' roses,
A pocket full o' posies.
A-tishoo! A-tishoo!
We all fall down.

Ring - a - ring o' ros - es, A pock - et full of po - sies. A-ti - shoo! A - ti - shoo! We all fall down.

Butterflies and Fish

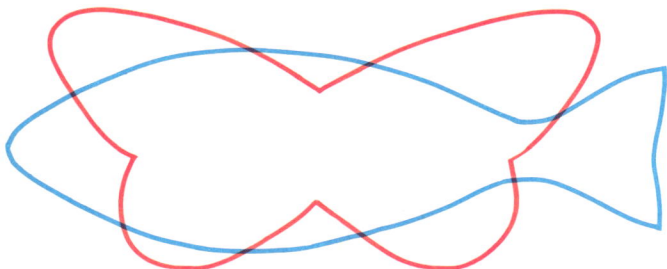

This game can be played both indoors and out (on a still day). Choose a different colour for each child and cut out six paper or card butterflies or fish in each colour. Place five of each colour in different positions round the house or garden. Then give each player his own fish or butterfly and send him off to find all the others exactly like it. At a given signal (or a set time) the winner will be the player who has found the most butterflies or fish of his own colour.

Musical Bumps

In its various forms, this can be played from the age of three upwards, both indoors and out.

You will need a record player or piano, cushions for every player but one, and one or two helpers.

Have a trial run to explain to the young guests what they have to do.

Place the cushions on the floor, not too close together so that each player has space to dance about. When the music stops each child has to find a cushion and 'bump' onto it. The one left standing is 'out'. Take away one cushion each time the music stops. When only two or three players are left, tell them to dance round two helpers to give each player more space (also there will be less likelihood of fights for the final places). The last one to 'bump' is the winner.

The Bunny Hop

Clear as much space as possible in the room. Tell the children that you would like them all to pretend they are rabbits. They know what rabbits do — they hop! Show them how they can hop like a rabbit — by squatting down and putting their hands on the floor between their knees. While the music is playing they must hop round the room, but as soon as it stops they must keep as still as possible. After a few rounds, a sweet can be given to each child 'because they are all so good' — or a winner can be found by eliminating those who topple over.

Squeak Piggy Squeak

All the players except one sit in a circle on the floor. The chosen player is then blindfolded and stands in the centre of the circle holding a cushion. She is taken round the circle until she says "Stop", and is then led to the nearest player. She places the cushion on the player's knee and sits down, saying "Squeak, piggy, squeak" as she does so. The player has to make a noise, and from this the blindfolded child has to guess whose knee she is sitting on. If she guesses correctly she changes places and the other child is blindfolded. If the guess is incorrect she must try again.

Grandmother's Footsteps

Children love this game, which will bring squeals of delight. One player chosen to be Grandmother stands at one end of the room or garden, with his or her back to the other players who form a line a given distance away. The object is to 'creep' up on Grandmother before she turns round. If she spins around and sees a player moving, that player must go back to the start and begin again. The one to touch Grandmother without being seen takes her place and the game starts again.

Hunt the Thimble

Everyone leaves the room except one person, who then hides the thimble. The thimble is hidden so that it can be seen without anything having to be moved. The other players return to the room for the search. When a child has discovered the thimble he or she sits down quietly. The last one to see it can hide it next time.

Blind Man's Buff

Although this is a very old game, it is still very popular with young children.

One of the children is chosen and is then blindfolded. The rest scatter, and the child who is blindfolded tries to catch one of them. When he does so, he must try to guess who the captive is by feeling her face and hair. If he guesses correctly, the one who has been caught is blindfolded.

Henny Penny

This is ideal to calm children down before tea.

You will need a one penny and a fivepence piece for every player, a cushion for each child, and the co-operation of other mothers.

Place a penny in the centre of each cushion, and tell the children to sit on them like mother hens. They must keep *very* still and quiet because they have got to 'hatch' their pennies into fivepence pieces! If one of the players becomes a little restive a mother can 'feel' to see if the penny has hatched, saying something like "Not quite, give it a little bit longer."

After a short interval the other mothers can 'feel' and substitute the coins, showing the little hens how clever they have been.

Dressing Up

Even the youngest child loves dressing up. Have a large box or basket of clothes containing at least one major garment for each child — include jackets and trousers as little boys often do not like dressing up as girls! Provide old hats, gloves, shoes, beads and scarves — let their imaginations run riot but *never* fail to recognise who they are supposed to be — the fairy queen or the lady next door.

Dressing up races can also be fun. Provide a similar number of garments for each child, and on the word 'Go', see who can get dressed first.

Hunt the Slipper

The players sit in a close circle, with one child sitting in the middle. She is given a slipper or shoe which she in turn hands to one of the children in the circle saying:

Cobbler cobbler mend my shoe
Have it done by half past two.

She then closes her eyes as the slipper is passed from player to player behind their backs while they say:

Cobbler cobbler tell me true
Which of you has got my shoe?

Whoever is holding the slipper when the word 'shoe' is said, keeps hold of it. The player in the middle then opens her eyes and must guess who is holding the slipper. If she guesses correctly the two players change places.

Treasure Hunt

To end the party, a simple treasure hunt can be easily organised.

Have ready long lengths of coloured wool (a different colour for each child) with small parcels wrapped in bright paper tied on at one end. Send the children out of the room for a moment and hide the parcels, then trail the lengths of wool round the room, ending near the door. Explain that this is not a race, and set the children off to find their own treasure.

Games
for FIVE
year olds

The Farmer's in his Den

All the children form a large circle, and walk round one child who has been chosen to be the farmer. They sing:

The farmer's in his den,
The farmer's in his den,
E – I – E – I,
The farmer's in his den.

The farmer wants a wife,
The farmer wants a wife,
E – I – E – I,
The farmer wants a wife.

Now the farmer chooses a wife to stand in the circle with him, and the game proceeds. The children sing the following verses, and at the end of each one, another child is chosen to stand in the circle.

The wife wants a child...

The child wants a nurse...

The nurse wants a dog...

The final verse is then sung:

We all pat the dog,
We all pat the dog,
E – I – E – I,
We all pat the dog.

Everyone playing the game then pats the dog on the head – gently!

The dog changes places with the farmer, and the game starts all over again.

The farm-er's in his den, the farm-er's in his den,

E - I - E - I, The farm-er's in his den.

Oranges and Lemons

Oranges and Lemons,
Say the bells of St Clement's;
You owe me five farthings,
Say the bells of St Martin's.
When will you pay me?
Say the bells of Old Bailey.
When I grow rich,
Say the bells of Shoreditch.
When will that be?
Say the bells of Stepney.
I'm sure I don't know,
Says the Great Bell of Bow.

Two tall children are chosen from the party, and stand facing each other, making an arch with their arms, at the top of the room. One becomes Orange, the other Lemon. Everyone sings the verse while the players form a long line, each holding the waist of the child in front and passing under the arch.

During the chorus:

> *Here comes a candle to light you to bed,*
> *Here comes a chopper to chop off your head!*

Orange and Lemon drop their arms at the word "Chop" catching the player passing beneath, who then has to choose which side to join. The game continues until all the players have been caught. At this stage there should be two almost equal teams and a tug-of-war ensues. The winners are the team to pull two or more of the opposing team over a marker placed on the floor.

Or-ang-es and lem-ons, say the bells of St. Cle-ment's, You

owe me five far-things say the bells of St. Mar-tin's;

When will you pay me? Say the bells of Old Bai-ley;

When I grow rich, Say the bells of Shore-ditch; When will that

be? Say the bells of Step-ney; I'm sure I don't know, says the

(Spoken)

Great Bell of Bow. Here comes a candle to light you to bed etc.

The Muffin Man

The Muffin Man is an older version of Blind Man's Buff. The players form a circle round the muffin man who is blindfolded and holds a walking stick (a ruler may be used).

The players dance round singing:

O, have you seen the muffin man,
The muffin man, the muffin man
O, have you seen the muffin man,
Who lives in Drury Lane?

At the last word everyone stands still. The player in the centre points the stick at someone, who must walk forward and take hold of it. The muffin man asks three questions, which should require only one word answers, for example:

"Do you like birthday cake?"
"Did you come to the party by car?"
"Are you wearing blue?"

The questions may be answered in a disguised voice and the muffin man is allowed three guesses to try to identify the player who is holding the stick. If one guess is correct, the two players change places.

O, have you seen the muf-fin man, The muf-fin man, the muf-fin man; O,

have you seen the muf-fin man Who lives in Dru-ry Lane O?

Musical Parcel

A small present is wrapped in a number of layers of paper, each layer tied up with string.

The players sit on the floor in a circle, and the parcel is given to one of them. The music starts, and the parcel is passed from child to child. When the music stops, the child who is holding the parcel unwraps as much of the paper and string as possible before the music starts again. The music is stopped at various intervals until the parcel is finally undone. The child who removes the final piece of paper wins the present.

Nosey

Divide the children into two teams. The leader of each team is given the outside covering of an ordinary matchbox which she places on her nose. She turns to the next player and the cover is then passed down the team from nose to nose (no hands are allowed) and back again. If the cover is dropped, it must be returned to the beginning to start again. The team whose leader receives the matchbox cover first is declared the winner.

Musical Hats

All the children sit round in a large circle. One child is given a hat to wear. When the music begins the hat is put onto the head of the next player, who in turn passes it onto the next. Whoever is wearing the hat when the music stops is 'out' and leaves the circle. The music starts again and the game continues until only one child is left who hasn't been 'caught' wearing the hat. He or she is declared the winner.

Poor Pussy

Ask the children to take up positions round the room pretending to be cats. They can curl up, kneel, go on all fours or sit on their heels. One player is chosen to be 'Mother' and she goes round to all the cats stroking them gently on the head or round the chin, saying "Poor Pussy". Pussy must try not to laugh, because if he does he has to change places and becomes Mother. The efforts of Pussy to keep a straight face will soon have everyone laughing.

Boys may prefer to be Lions!

Plate Race

You will need a good supply of paper plates for this game. Divide the children into two teams (more if there are enough children). Mark out two lines for the start and finish, a reasonable distance apart. Give each team leader two plates which she puts side by side on the starting line. They then have to 'walk' their plates to the finish. To do this they have to stand on one plate and pick up the second plate, placing it a step in front, without letting the second foot touch the ground. Balance is all important! As soon as one member of the team has finished, the next should start, with a new pair of plates!

Animal Tails or Ears

Although this game needs a certain amount of preparation, it will evoke gales of laughter. Draw the outline of an animal on a large sheet of paper or card and fix this firmly on to a strong board. The animal you choose depends on how artistic you are (a donkey is popular), and it is as well to have one or two spares in case one gets torn. Make a drawing of the tail or ears (larger than they would be to be in proportion), and cut these from fairly stiff paper – cartridge paper is ideal. Put a small piece of 'Blu-tack' on the back of the tail or ears (to attach it to the main drawing of the animal).

Give each player an ear or tail (with his name marked on it), and tell him to hold it at a point near the 'Blu-tack'. Let the child take a good look at the animal before putting on a blindfold. Then set him off in a straight line towards the animal, where he has to fix the tail in the correct position. Shouts of laughter will greet each attempt!

The winner is the one nearest 'the mark'.

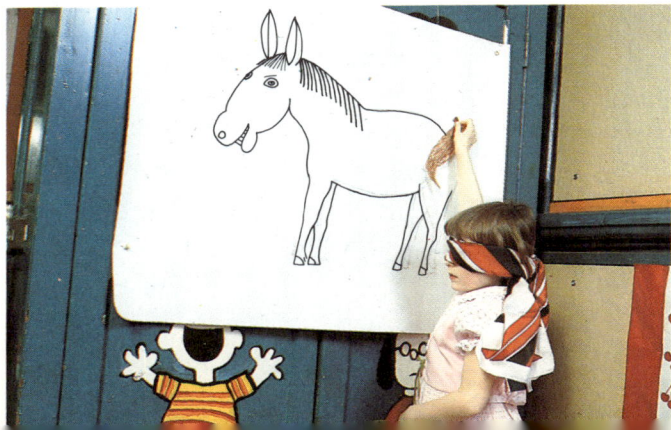

Pushing a Pig

A team game which will need a sausage-shaped balloon and either a walking stick or an umbrella for each team. The balloon may be made to look more realistic by drawing (with a felt tipped pen) two eyes and two large ears at one end, and a curly tail at the other. (Have some spares available.) The players stand behind a starting line, with a further line about 3 metres (10 feet) away.

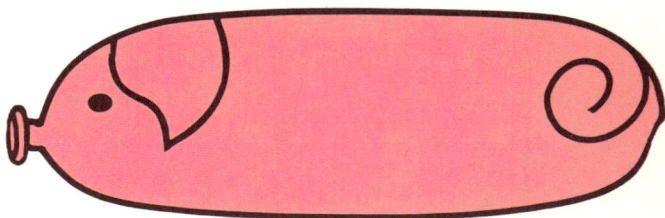

The first player from each team stands up to the line with the 'pig' on the floor by his feet, holding the stick in his hand. At the word "Go", he pushes the pig forward with the stick. He is allowed to tap either end, but not in the middle. The idea is to push the pig across the far line and back again to the starting place.

The second member then takes over following the same course. The game continues until all the players have completed the course. The first team to do so are the winners.

Blow Feather

This game has to be played indoors. Form the players into two teams facing each other. Have a stock of good-sized (but not heavy) feathers ready. The object is to keep the feathers in the air. The first member of one team blows it to the first member of the other team, who in turn must blow it back to the second member of the first team, zig-zag fashion. Any team member who allows the feather to fall is given a penalty point. The winners are the team with the *least* points.

Straw Ball

Another blowing game, but quite different from the last. It can be played as a race, in a large room or out of doors, with heats to find the winner, or as a team game.

The players are asked to go down on their hands and knees at the start line with the straw in their mouths. A ping pong ball is placed before each player, and on the word 'Go' they have to crawl forwards, gently blowing the ball towards the finish. On a polished floor the ball will roll away quickly with only a gentle 'puff', but on carpet or grass it will need a slightly harder 'blow'.

Flipping a Kipper

Any age that can 'flip' can play. First prepare a few kippers! These can be cut out of newspaper or thin card, as shown in the sketch. You will also need some folded copies of a daily newspaper. The players form two teams, then you place a kipper on the floor in front of the leader; he then has to 'flip' it gently, in a fanning manner, to the finish line. Spare kippers and fans will probably be needed.

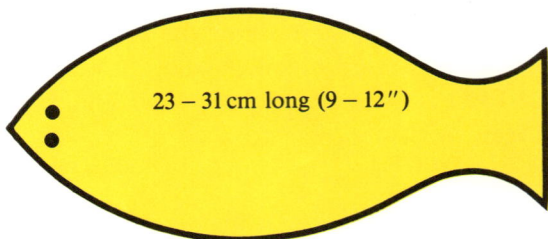

23 – 31 cm long (9 – 12″)

Games
for SIX to
SEVEN and
upwards

London Bridge

Two children form an arch, the others running beneath, holding each other round the waist, at the same time singing the verses.

1 *London Bridge is falling down,*
   Falling down, falling down,
   London Bridge is falling down,
   My fair lady.

2 *Build it up with iron bars,*
   Iron bars, iron bars,
   Build it up with iron bars,
   My fair lady.

3 *Iron bars will bend and bow, etc.*

4 *Build it up with pins and needles, etc.*

5 *Pins and needles will rust and bend, etc.*

6 *Build it up with penny loaves, etc.*

7 *Penny loaves will tumble down, etc.*

8 *Here's a prisoner I have got, etc.*

9 *What's the prisoner done to you, etc.*

10 *Stole my watch and broke my chain, etc.*

11 *What'll you take to set him free, etc.*

12 *Ten hundred pounds will set him free, etc.*

13 *Ten hundred pounds we have not got, etc.*

14 *Then off to prison he must go, etc.*

At verse 8 the 'arch' must catch a prisoner, and lead him out of the game at verse 14. The song begins again, but can be shortened. The last two in the line become the arch, the two original players joining the front of the line. With the loss of the prisoners, speed is essential not to get caught. The game can become rough without careful supervision!

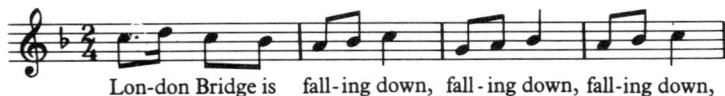

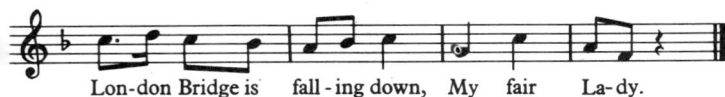

Lon-don Bridge is   fall-ing down, fall-ing down, fall-ing down,

Lon-don Bridge is   fall-ing down,   My   fair   La-dy.

O'Grady Says...

A game which causes endless amusement. One of the players is nominated as O'Grady, and from now on his orders must be obeyed. The children line up before him and he may say "O'Grady says, stand on one leg", and everyone must stand on one leg. "O'Grady says, put the leg down" – everyone puts their leg down to the floor again. Should he say "Hands up" without saying "O'Grady says..." to start with, any player raising his hands is out. The faster the game is played, the more hilarious it becomes.

As an alternative to being 'out', all those players who made mistakes during the game can be made to pay a forfeit (for example, sing a song).

Musical Statues

Have ready a number of helpers and a fairly fast piece of pop music, so that the children can disco dance.

Before starting tell the dancers that when the music stops they must take up special positions, and stay absolutely still. Give them three or four alternatives such as a soldier, jockey, tennis player or ballet dancer. Anyone seen to wobble, or laugh, is out.

Crossing the River

Older children enjoy this game; it requires a lot of energy!

Although not strictly a team game, it is best to divide the players into equal numbers. Explain that certain parts of the room, or lawn, are the banks of a river. When the music starts the players must run or jump to the opposite 'bank'. Should the music stop when they are in 'mid-stream', they are out. The last person to 'keep his feet dry' is the winner.

Animal Noises

A boisterous way to find a partner!

The children are told individually, and very quietly, the name of an animal − a cow, dog, sheep or donkey, for example. Two children are allotted to each animal, and are told to find their partner by making the appropriate noise of their particular animal. If you include a rabbit, this will add to the fun – they just wrinkle their noses! This is a good way to 'break the ice' at the start of a party.

Busy Bees

For this game you will need an 'odd man out', all the other players having a partner. The 'odd man' becomes the leader and stands alone while the pairs spread out. Then the leader calls out commands: "Stand side to side", "Stand back to back", "Face each other", and the pairs of children must obey the orders. But when the leader shouts "Busy Bees", everyone must choose a new partner. The leader joins in, and whoever is left without a partner becomes the new leader.

The Postman

This is best played out of doors or in a large room. A little preparation is required.

Enlist the help of a friendly shoe shop for some empty boxes with lids. Fasten the lids on securely with adhesive tape, and paint a distinctive shape and colour on each box: an orange square, a green circle, a blue diamond, a yellow oblong, and so on. Four or six boxes are usually enough for a party of ten or twelve children. Cut a slit in the top of the lid big enough to take half a postcard. Prepare cards that will easily fit through the slots (you will need about ten cards per child). Stick on (or paint) on the cards an even number of coloured shapes to match the boxes. Hide the boxes so that the players have to *look* for them.

To start the game give each child a card with a coloured shape on it, jot her name on the reverse, and send her to 'post' the letter in the appropriate box. Each time a player returns send her off again with a different coloured shape (don't forget to put her name on the back).

For those children who can read, the boxes can have names with matching cards, for example CREWE, LONDON, EXETER and BATH.

After a set time stop the game and open all the boxes. The winner is the player with the greatest number of posted cards, in the correct boxes!

Two Hats

All the children except one sit in a row. The remaining child is then given two hats, one of which she wears. As she walks along the row she chooses another player and gives her the second hat. Now this player must do everything contrary to the child in the first hat. If she puts on her hat, the other keeps it off. If she holds it in her right hand, the other holds it in her left; if she sits down, the other stands up. This continues until a mistake is made, whereupon the players change places and another 'victim' is chosen.

Hot and Cold

A thimble or small ornament is chosen and shown to the children. One player is then asked to leave the room, while the others hide the object. The child returns to the room and begins to search. If he is near the object the others shout "Getting warmer", but if he moves away they shout "Getting colder", until the article is found.

Looby Loo

The children form a circle and perform the actions as they sing:

Here we go looby loo,
Here we go looby light,
Here we go looby loo
All on a Saturday night.

You put your right arm in
You put your right arm out
You shake it a little, a little,
And turn yourself about.

Do the same with

You put your left arm in

You put your both arms in

You put your right foot in

You put your left foot in

You put your both feet in

Finally

You put your whole self in
You put your whole self out
You shake it a little, a little,
And turn yourself about.

Here we go Loo - by Loo, Here we go Loo - by Light,

Here we go Loo - by Loo, All on a Sa-tur-day night. You

put your right arm in————, You put your right arm out

Plate and Marble Race

Players are divided into two teams. The leader of each is given a plate containing five or six marbles. For younger children, small dishes may be used instead of shallow plates. The plate then passes from the leader overhead to the next player, and so on down the line until the last player receives the plate of marbles. He then races to the front and the plate is again passed overhead as before. The race continues until the original leader once more becomes the first member of the team. If any marbles are dropped they must be replaced and the plate must not be moved until the number is correct.

To make the race more difficult, the plate may be passed alternately under the legs and then over the heads, down the line.

Front and Back Race

You will need two saucers holding about twelve items such as shells, buttons, beans, etc., one for each team. Teams of equal numbers stand in line and by the leader of each are placed the two saucers, one full and the other empty.

At the word "Go" the leader picks up one object and passes it on to the next child in the line, who passes it on again, until the object reaches the last player. The object is then passed back up the line —

only this time it is handed along behind everyone's back. Simultaneously the leader picks up another object and passes it on. Thus objects are passing up and down the line at the same time in front and behind the backs of the players.

As the leader receives each object it is placed in the empty saucer until all the items have been transferred from one saucer to the other. The leader must count the objects so that he knows when the race has been completed and can raise his hand to have his team declared the winner.

Balloon Knees

This game can be played either indoors or out, either as a race or a team game, depending on the number of players.

For a race, line up the contestants and give each a round balloon. This is placed between the knees, and on the word "Go" the children walk as fast as they can to the finish line, without dropping the balloon. This is not as easy as it sounds!

The team game is played in a similar manner, but on reaching the finish line the leader picks up the balloon and runs back to the next member. The winning team is the one whose leader returns to the top of the line first.

Chin~Chin

A simple team game suitable for most ages. Divide the children into two teams standing in line. The leader of each team is given a large apple or orange to place under his or her chin. At the command "Go", the orange must be passed to the next member of the team, without using hands, but passing from chin to chin.

If the orange drops on the floor, the *passer* must pick it up and not the person receiving it.

A variation of this is *Spoon Ball.* Played as before but you will need a spoon for each team member who must place the handle in his or her mouth. The team leaders are then given a ping-pong ball in their spoons which must be passed down the line from spoon to spoon. Again hands must not be used, and it is disastrous to laugh!

Puzzle Pictures

Collect a large number of brightly coloured birthday and Christmas cards, or pictures from magazines. Cut each in half, at different angles, keeping the two halves in separate piles. Distribute one set round the rooms or garden. Give each competitor one of the halves to try to match it up and make a complete picture again. The winner is the one who collects the most correct pictures. Be very careful to keep a list of names with the number of pictures collected marked against each.

A~tissue

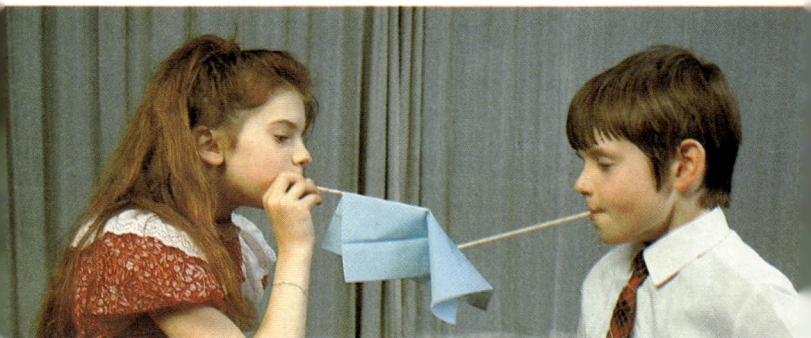

You will require a piece of tissue paper for each team (have some spares ready as well) and a straw for each player.

Ask the children to choose two teams. Give the leader of each team a piece of tissue paper approximately 15 cm (6 in) square to place over the top of her straw. She puts the other end of the straw into her mouth and draws a deep breath, thus keeping the tissue paper on the end of the straw.

Turning to the next member of the team, she slowly lets out her breath, releasing the paper; the next player draws in a breath, and the paper is transferred from one straw to the next. The paper passes down the line in this way, and the first team to finish are the winners.

If the tissue paper falls to the floor, the person who allows it to fall may pick it up with her hand and replace it on the end of her straw.

Wrong~handed Drawing

The children are divided into two teams and each team is given paper and pencils. One player from each team is told in secret the name of a familiar object. She returns to her team and attempts to draw the object, using her 'wrong' hand.

The rest of the team try to guess what it is, but the child who has drawn the object may only answer their guesses by saying "Yes" or "No". The children must talk quietly or the other team may hear their answer. The player who guesses correctly takes out their answer and is told the next object to draw. The winning team is the one to guess all the drawings correctly.

A variation for older children could be to draw Nursery Rhymes, or simple book titles.

Consequence Drawing

Each child is given a piece of paper and a pencil. Beginning at the top of the paper, they are asked to draw a head and a neck, for example a policeman, a deep sea diver or a lady in a flowery hat. It is important not to let the other children see what each child has drawn. The paper is then folded over, with two lines for the neck showing, and passed on to the next player. This time a body, arms and the beginning of the legs are added, the papers are folded and passed on. Finally, legs and feet are drawn. The papers are unfolded and the bodies revealed. The results usually cause much amusement, especially to younger children.

Objects on a Tray

Each player will need a piece of paper and a pencil. A tray will have to be prepared beforehand and remain hidden until the game is ready to be played.

A number of objects — about twelve — are placed on the tray; for example, an egg cup, comb, key, pencil, salt pot, hair slide and thimble. The tray is then covered.

When everyone is ready the tray is uncovered and the children allowed a few minutes to remember the objects. The tray is then covered again and the children write down as many objects as they can remember. The one with the highest number wins.

For *Mystery Objects*, a little preparation is also needed. Place a number of objects of differing sizes and shapes in a pillow case, and loosely sew up the end. For the game the children are allowed a specified time to 'feel' and try to identify the various items. After a time they write down their answers, the pillow case is opened, and again the player with highest number of correct objects is the winner.

What you will need

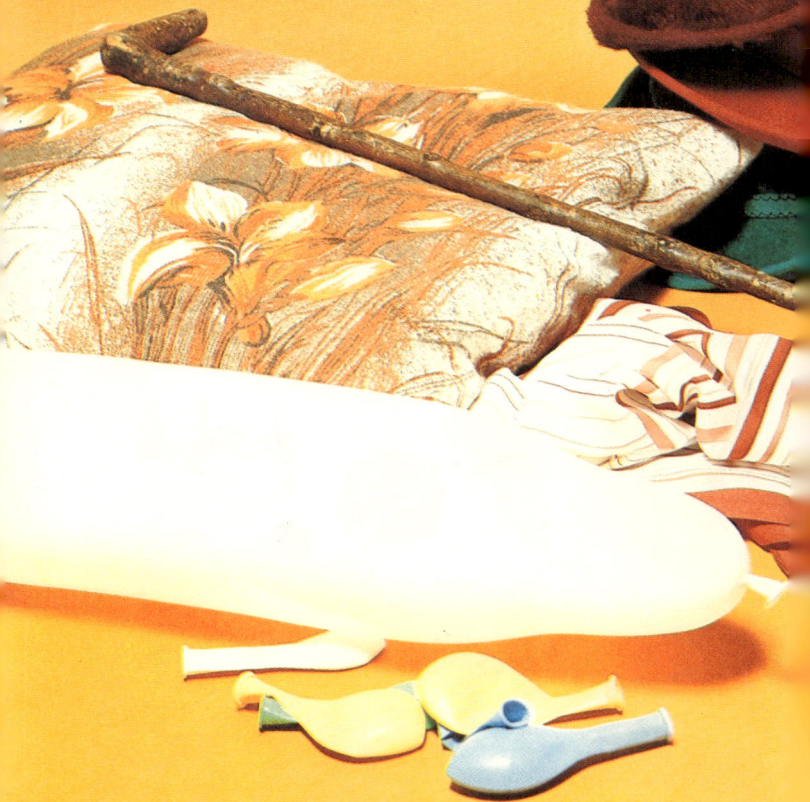